THE
MISSING
RED
LETTERS

MARK T. BARCLAY

MARK BARCLAY
PUBLICATIONS

2010 N. Stark Road • Midland, MI 48642-9439

The Missing Red Letters

ISBN 978-0-944802-58-8

Copyright © 2014 Mark T. Barclay

Published by Mark Barclay Publications

Mark Barclay Ministries

2010 N. Stark Road, Midland, MI 48642-9439

www.marktbarclay.com

MARK BARCLAY PUBLICATIONS

2010 N. Stark Road • Midland, MI 48642-9439

Contents

Introduction

Why, in such a great nation, do we have shootings in our schools, our places of business, and even our churches?

There is an extremely wicked, dangerous, and lethal plan unfolding right before our very eyes. What is it? An orchestrated attack against the two most crucial documents that liberate man and allow him his God-given rights and freedoms. They are parallel. They are the Constitution of the United States with its Bill of Rights, and the Word of God (the Holy Scriptures).

It's so strange to me that it isn't outside enemies who seem to be attacking either of these; it's from within. It isn't so much other nations attacking our documents of rights and freedoms; it's Americans. And it isn't so much the blatant sinner who is attacking the Holy Scriptures; it is actually many of our popular evangelical speakers.

For example, I've heard the Bible attacked from the pulpits, telecasts, writings, and social media. Things like, "The Bible is not for today," or "It's out of touch with modern man." I've even heard instruction from some of the most famous speakers to eliminate and not read certain books of the Bible, including 1 John, the entire Old Testament, and even the red letters. I say nonsense and ridiculous! In fact, we need more Word, not less.

It just hasn't been that long ago that my generation actually attended high school and college. Yes, sin and rebellion existed, yet we faced little to none of these evil, treacherous events and horrible life-damaging attacks.

Not too many years ago, our news was not as filled with missing teenagers and young children. Neither were entire families being murdered and so many humans raped and abused as today. Well, certainly not in the United States of America.

Sure, we had our crime, and as with every generation, we had our crises. But it was not at all to the severity level that it is now. I cannot believe the terrible things that humans do to humans today. Furthermore, it's getting so common to hear about violence and filthy penetrations of privacy that you can hardly tell whom you can and cannot trust.

Man does not seem to be able to fix these problems. I encourage everyone—parents, teachers, law enforcement, the judicial system, all the way to our White House—to keep trying to do something to protect us. However, it seems as though they do not possess the authority or wisdom to bring resolution. Not to discourage you, but it seems like man's efforts are failing. Yet even in this great "Christian" nation, we do not turn to God and live the way He teaches us to live. Could it be that the greatest underlying problem and the real disturbing truth is we have swayed away from the teachings of the Lord Jesus Christ?

In this book, I plan to discuss some of these teachings, for they cover almost every walk of life. There is probably nothing you can name for which Jesus Christ does not have an answer in the red letters of your Bible. I learned many years ago that the Word of the Lord is not just for "church" but everyday life. The Word of God works all night long and all day long for those who work it. God is not just interested in making you a blue-ribbon sheep or a gold-star church attendee. We come to the house of the Lord to study the Word of the Lord and learn how to live according to the teachings of our Lord and Savior, Jesus Christ, so when we step out of the church building and enter back into the activities of life, we can conquer the hindrances and attacks against us.

I tell you, there is nothing you will face in this life that is not covered by the Holy Scriptures. In these powerful Words of Christ (the red letters), every issue of life is addressed in one way or another. In the chapters to follow, you will see that Jesus covered family, wages, violations, the law, supply, friends, your neighbor, and yes, even your enemies . . . and much more.

In this book, I present to you the heart-wrenching fact that it is the missing red letters causing our problems. It is the absence of the teachings of Jesus Christ that has slowly turned the great United States of America (the only nation ever established on purpose to be a Christian nation) to become so anti-Christ. It is this anti-Christ spirit spreading intolerance toward Jesus and His Church that is causing our society to deteriorate at such a fast rate. In fact, I would compare it to a runaway locomotive. That's why even our young people (who seldom hear these great red letters, let alone be raised by them) walk in such rebellion, hatred, anger, and devilish ways. I am not just speaking from a religious platform but as a citizen of the United States and a fellow human, fighting my way through these great last days.

Someone asked me, "What is the fix to all this, Brother Barclay? Who can bring the real healing and solution?" You and I know it is ultimately the Lord Jesus Christ Himself, His Word, and those who preach it with the proper motive and the boldness of our Master Himself. But I also believe with all my heart it is our parents and our teachers who hold our future in their hands. Why do I say this? Because of all the people in our children's lives, no one has more time with them than the teachers and parents. If the teachers and parents are anti-Christ and do not teach our wonderful Christian American history from its proper standpoint, our children will not turn out to be the strong, courageous, honest, and forgiving people we want them to be. As we enter into my book, *The Missing Red Letters*, let's be reminded that our young people are the next judges (including Supreme Court judges), lawmakers, teachers, and so on.

You can claim I am a Jesus fanatic, or far religious right, or too spiritually minded to be any earthly good, or just plain out of touch with real life. My challenge to you is to read the powerful red letters in the Bible, and you will easily see the solutions to today's perilous times. This is true, no matter your denomination. In fact, it is true even if you are not a churchgoer. Answers are answers, and solutions are solutions, whether you are a religious person or not.

We must stop denying our children the teachings and lifestyle of our Lord and Savior, Jesus Christ. We must go back to our true American history, which clearly proclaims we are a Christian nation and that Jehovah is our God. This makes Jesus Christ our Savior and the Lord of our life. Therefore we should be raising our children after the teachings of Christ.

I challenge us to do this for a generation and see it repel the wickedness and filth, which are ruling our nation. There are reasons why there are scriptural quotations throughout our government buildings and our history books, as well as recorded prayers from some of the greatest men and women who have formed and led this great nation.

What on earth has happened to us? Why is there such hatred toward Jesus Christ and His people in these days? Why is there so much willingness to pull away from our roots and consequently continue to live in such horrible pain, fear, soulful torture, and violence?

The answers are in the great Words of Jesus Christ—the red letters of the Bible—which I have identified in red ink here in this book to bring honor and emphasis.

1

The Missing Red Letters Dilemma

As I travel around the world, preaching the gospel to the lost and teaching the body of Christ, I find a real shortage of the "red letters." Let me explain. In a Red Letter Edition Bible, the Words of Christ are all printed with red ink and thus referred to as the "red letters."

These red letters, the Words and teachings of Jesus Christ, are among the least taught messages of the Bible truths today. It seems that even the Pauline epistles are more popular than Jesus' teachings.

I understand that all scripture is God-breathed or inspired by Him. Yes, I understand that the Pauline epistles, as well as the rest of the Bible, are indeed the Words of our God. Our God is a three-part being (Father, Son, and Holy Spirit) yet one God. The Holy Spirit is the author of the entire Bible and used men who walked the earth to put it on tablets or scrolls. You could say they were His secretaries.

2 TIMOTHY 3:16-17

> All scripture is given by inspiration of God, and is profitable for doctrine, for reproof, for correction, for instruction in righteousness: That the man of God may be perfect, thoroughly furnished unto all good works.

We are to study the entire Bible and have all the Words of God in us. We are to study them and totally live by them. The Bible is referred to as a two-edged sword, the Old and New Testaments. But it is also expected of us to allow the Words of "Christ" to dwell in us "richly."

COLOSSIANS 3:16

> Let the word of Christ dwell in you richly in all wisdom; teaching and admonishing one another in psalms and hymns and spiritual songs, singing with grace in your hearts to the Lord.

In this book, I want to emphasize how important it is to study the teachings of our Lord and Savior, Jesus Christ. Let all the Word of God dwell in you, but let the Words of Christ dwell in you "richly." Please don't misunderstand what I am saying here. I love the whole Bible, and I teach the whole Bible, from Genesis to Revelation. I study, preach, teach, and meditate in the Word of God; but I have made it one of my goals in life to know the teachings of Jesus more than any other teaching, and to know the red letters better than any other scriptures.

It is Jesus who is my Savior, and He is the Head of the Church. As a New Testament believer, I am to submit to my Lord Jesus and live His lifestyle as I abandon mine. As a full-time gospel minister, I am to submit to Him as my Commander and Chief and carry out His decrees, as well as fulfill His ministry in the earth.

It is Jesus we love and to whom we belong. His desire for our life is our greatest desire and the one to which we "sell out." He is the great Master Teacher, and His truths should live in us. We should know them better than the teachings of any modern man or author. As a matter of fact, it is more important that we know Jesus and His life and times more thoroughly and intimately than any other Bible character.

Back to the dilemma, as I travel around the body of Christ (which I do somewhere almost every day), I can't help but notice the lack of teaching and discussion about Jesus. Not to seem like

I'm nitpicking, but many overuse the name "Holy Spirit" and "Father God" rather than speak of Jesus. How long has it been since you heard a minister holding a seminar on sheep and goats, or wheat and tares? How about a teaching on selling all you have and following Him, or one on the unjust servant? It is very hard to find a seminar or conference on right living or avoiding sin, lust, and the world. Jesus taught on all these things and many other truths that we seldom hear today.

Why is this so important? Because we have an entire generation of Christians who don't know Him or what He stands for. Many Christians can't tell you the convictions and principles for which Jesus was persecuted and eventually crucified. We must turn the body of Christ back to Jesus and saturate them with His teachings and His presence.

As I mentioned in the introduction of this book, we have a severe problem. It's like a runaway locomotive. Society is out of control. And with all our great laws and lawmakers, we cannot seem to enforce the issues of safety, protection, and the peaceful pursuit of happiness. As Americans we often refer to this great pursuit of happiness and this wonderful "freedom." Not to be negative, but isn't this slipping away from us at a rapid pace?

And another question, why do we want the word "God" removed from everything? What's this all about? First we want it and everything about it removed from our schools, then our courthouses and other public buildings, and eventually we will want it removed from our currency and our Pledge of Allegiance.

Who raised this perverse generation? Who taught them they can live without the help of the Almighty God? And why are they so blind? What has such a grip on their mind that they want to continue living this way, under these conditions, and with all this fear?

I realize the Bible warns us that this misbehavior will absolutely be a part of last-days living. I have mentioned this in several books I've written over the years. I explain it thoroughly in my book, *Things You Need for the Day Ahead*, but for reference purposes here, let me remind you that Jesus predicted our day (the last days) to be a day like Noah's day and a day like Lot's day. In other words, a day of partying, sexual perversion, and a carefree attitude about the things of life and the future—that is, until judgment came, and it was too late for almost everyone.

I know deep within me that as judgment falls upon the earth, people will once again be living any way they want to, even mocking our God and those who preach His Word. It will, without a doubt, surprise some like a thief in the night. But then again, if they were reading the red letters of their Bible, they would know to be prepared for it and therefore be preserved.

I do not believe at all that I am exaggerating the condition of society. If anything, I am not reporting this as thoroughly as I could for the sake of not making anyone look and feel any worse.

When our society allowed prosperity, pretense, and the entertainment industry to mock the biblical roles of life, it was like waving the white flag of surrender. We now have a whole generation of people (maybe two) who do not reverence God or the things that are taught from His Holy Book. Instead, they are being raised on video games, violent movies that have no respect for life, and the idea that if you don't like somebody you can shoot them or blow them up.

It is no longer about having enough to eat, proper clothing, or good health. It is now all about the insignia on the clothing, the designer jeans, and "putting on the Ritz"—whether you can afford it or not. It is clear that the goal now has to do with what we look like and little to do with honesty, hard work, or personal achievement. We can deceive many with our facade, pretense, and showmanship.

World history proves that people with this goal and these low morals eventually destroy themselves. America (though the only nation on the planet established for Christian purposes and freedoms) is not the only nation that grew powerful, with strong military might, and influenced the world. But I ask you today, where are these great nations? Where are these influential people? Why do they and their empires comprise only a portion of our history books? What on earth happened to these people?

I'm telling you, this is the dilemma. Even many of our preachers today are not convicted to live according to the Word of God. Many of them do not truly preach the Word of God. Many of those who have a great platform and a massive audience want to be motivational speakers rather than preachers of the Word of God. The truth is, it's a lack of good preaching and a lack of the conviction that comes from it that has hurt our great nation the most.

The dilemma is the struggle of getting the red letters back in the pulpits of America, back in the history books of America, back in the heart of all Americans. When we have preachers, pulpiteers, and church leaders who purposely avoid the teachings of Jesus Christ (because they fear it will be offensive to the average person who is living in sin), how will we ever change this nation?

Honesty, integrity, forgiveness, going the extra mile to help another, generosity, joy, health, and peace of mind are all by-products of the teachings of the Lord Jesus Christ. To tell a rapist not to rape is not going to work. To lock up a rapist and tell him not to rape is not going to work either. But changing one from the powers of darkness to the powers of light could make all the difference in not only the rapist's life but every potential future victim.

To say the murderer will go away if you remove all the handguns is not going to work. Can I please remind you that history has already proven this? Cain, the brother of Abel, killed him. He had no gun. No, I am not speaking for any gun advocate organization or anyone else. I'm just smart enough to know that if you remove the guns, you'll still have murders. You will still have murders because you will still have murderers. Then they will go to knives, and when you remove all the knives, there will still be murders because there will still be murderers. And when they pick up sticks and stones to kill one another, and you remove all the sticks and stones from the earth, there will still be murders because there will still be murderers.

Again, the red letters of our Bible tell us that murdering is a heart issue, and unless you change the heart of the murderer, he or she will find a way to do it again. "For out of the heart proceed evil thoughts, murders, adulteries, fornications, thefts, false witness, blasphemies . . ." (Matt. 15:19). Jesus Christ is the only One who can take the heart of the murderer or any other violent person and change them forever and ever and ever.

Let's bring this back to the local church. Even in the modern churches, most Christians are living a lifestyle that does not line up to the biblical New Testament expectation. I truly believe that a dirty church is a powerless church. Sin absolutely steals our confidence and our boldness in Christ. Absolutely, without a doubt, living a sinful life quenches the great Holy Spirit, who is the power of this gospel.

The entire Bible gives reverence to holiness, an upright heart, clean hands, a pure heart, and a separation from the old life. Even so, almost every story Jesus told was to either direct us to live in this world with a Kingdom lifestyle, or warn us of what happens to those who don't. Parable after parable, Jesus brings us clarity, insight, warnings, and directions. With such an absence of the red letters in our preaching and sermons today, we are walking away from not only the requirements of Christianity but also the restriction it places on our heart.

There is a philosophy, a humanistic desire, that is as old as mankind to live any way I want to, say what I want, do what I want, with whomever I want, and still have the blessing of the Lord on my life and make Heaven. However, the true record shows that no one has ever lived such a way under the permission of God. It also shows that those men who wanted to do things their own way rather than God's way ended up not only in trouble with God but in great difficulties in their own personal lives. As a matter of fact, some actually died.

I believe with all my heart there is only one way out of this fix we're in, and that is to get back to the teachings of our Savior, Jesus Christ, and walk them out. I do not believe we will ever see the end of total darkness and evil spirits, and I suppose as long as there is a thing called a man, we will have to contend with foolishness. Even so, until the absolute end of the age, Jesus Christ will hold the keys to hell and the grave, with the ability to set us free from every enemy force.

As we, the Church, get back to the Book, live in the red letters, and do what they say; our power will return, our confidence will return, and we will once again live under great conviction. This is a *good* thing! If you want to know more about conviction and our conscience and why we have one, please get my book, *Things You Need for the Day Ahead*, where I dedicate an entire chapter to this topic.

Obviously the great beauty of reading and studying the Bible's red letters is that they're actually the Words of our Christ, but they also reveal the heart of our Christ. If you want to know Jesus Christ and what He taught, live in the red letters.

Let's venture into the rest of the chapters of this book and discover the great missing link to the greatest life anyone has ever offered—a life filled with love, power, peace, and a great inner joy; a life of success and accomplishment; and a life of dreams come true.

PHILIPPIANS 3:10

> That I may know him, and the power of his resurrection, and the fellowship of his sufferings, being made conformable unto his death . . .

2

The Gospel According to Jesus

One of the reasons I am writing this book is to expose the difference between Jesus' preaching and modern-day preaching. I understand there are many different kinds of preachers and different levels of maturity and even different depths of spirituality. This is true with both the preacher and the listener.

No matter whom we compare, we will come far short of the exact duplicate of Jesus' messages. None of us preachers will ever become so eloquent in speech that we can even come close to Jesus. However, we should at least strive to re-preach His sermons and share the heart of "His" gospel in our messages.

When Jesus preached, He covered all areas of life. He was a master communicator. He was also a master at confronting people and pointing out their sins and self-afflictions—not to their hurt but to lead them to repentance and deliverance.

Jesus dealt with different people in different ways. He was very compassionate toward the sick, poor, hurting, and shepherdless. He was demanding with His disciples and very stern with the religious. He gave great grace to those who were spiritually hungry and drove others from the temple. He gave Pharisees and Sadducees a hard time, yet He would stop the whole meeting just to touch one person. He basically told the rich young ruler to get in all the way or get lost, but He went across the entire body of water to set one man free.

Was Jesus confrontational at all? Yes, emphatically yes. Was He outside of love while doing this? No, absolutely not. In today's church, which seems mostly self-seeking and self-promoting, any confrontation is labeled as "no love" or "no shepherd's heart." "Where is the love of Jesus?" they will say.

I am not sure Jesus would be very popular if He were born in this day rather than the days of old. I don't think most pastors would invite Him to speak in their churches and would probably be almost terrified of the people's response to His messages. The Church seems to have drifted far away from Christ's style and His message and leaned more toward a message filled with humanism, self-gain, and soulful soothing.

Too critical for you? Let's get back to Jesus. Our Master is also our master model. His lifestyle, ministry style, message style, message content, and His entire life should be our master model. This is especially true for us preachers.

This is not our message; it is His. This is not our Kingdom; it is His. It is not our flock; it is His. It is not our job, duty, call, or assignment in life to create a gospel that is palatable to the deteriorating standards of society. It is rather to preach His Word and carry His message to the very ends of the earth until the very end of our life. Think it not strange, for those preachers who worked before us have done the same.

Our preaching should sound like Jesus' preaching. Our sermons should be Jesus' sermons; our message, His message; and our principles, His principles. Our countenance, expressions, and communication style should be filled with Jesus. When people hear us, they should hear Jesus. When we stand to preach, we should be thinking about our Master and how we can please Him and draw others to Him.

I am not talking about becoming "Jesus only" and ignoring the Father and His Spirit. I am simply saying that He is every true preacher's boss, as well as the supplier of truth. We are His deputies, and we must deliver His message to mankind and fulfill His ministry in the earth. No man has the right to use the pulpit or the church to communicate his own message or accomplish his own goals. This is not about us; it is about Jesus. We are to decrease, and He is to increase.

Consider these examples of how Jesus expressed the gospel:

Jesus was the preacher who was known for His boldness and authority (Matt. 7:28-29).

Jesus was the preacher who confronted the woman at the well, revealing her sins (Jn. 4:6-19).

Jesus was the preacher who called the Pharisees names in a public service while they were actually present (Matt. 23:13-33).

Jesus was the preacher who told one of His most prominent disciples to get behind Him and even called him satan. This also was done in front of the others (Matt. 16:21-24).

Jesus was the preacher who made a whip and cleansed the temple. He actually pushed over tables and ran people out of the church (Jn. 2:15-16).

Jesus was the preacher who was found boldly preaching the message of the Kingdom and dealing face to face with religious confronters (Lk. 13:14-17).

Jesus was the preacher who set Pilate straight during His court case (Jn. 19:10-11).

Jesus was the preacher who warned His weeping followers to weep for themselves and for their children, not for Him (Lk. 23:28-30).

Among Jesus' great mastery collection of teachings are the golden ones that follow:

- Forgive seventy times seven in one day.
- The unjust servant, turned over to the tormentors to pay the full price.
- Sheep go to Heaven, and goats to hell.
- A hireling preacher runs when trouble comes.
- Beware of even a little leaven (man's religion, philosophy, and sin).
- The three unacceptable excuses.
- The five virgins who lost out on eternal life.
- The fifty percent factor (see my book, *The Remnant Church*).
- Deny yourself.
- Put Me first, or you cannot be My disciple (leave father, mother, etc.).
- Wolves in sheep's clothing.
- Go and sin no more, lest something worse happens to you.

Let's look a little closer to discover how intense Jesus really was about His message and assignment on the earth.

SHEEP GO TO HEAVEN—GOATS TO HELL

This is a classic. Too bad you don't hear this preached very often anymore. Many people would live much cleaner lives and stay much closer to Christ if they did. For some reason, people become what they hear most.

If they live on a diet of hearing the benefits of Jesus preached, they will be in love with the benefits and seek the benefits. If they live on a diet of hearing the person and lifestyle of Christ preached, they will fall in love with Jesus and want His lifestyle.

I am shocked at how many people today don't even know most of the gospel story or what Jesus expects of them. As I travel around this world and walk among the churches, I discover just how little the average Christian reads the Bible, especially those verses about how Jesus dealt with the things of life.

This story of the sheep and goats is not just a warning or confrontation. It is a shepherd (the Good Shepherd) crying out to us to live the life and walk the walk. People usually don't like it when we preach from these verses. Why? I suppose it's because it causes us to soul search and examine our way of life.

Did you know that when the angels come they will separate the sheep from the goats, and it will be based on life performance? No, I am not at all talking about working your way to Heaven or being justified by your works. However, it is the rule of Heaven that whatever a man believes, that is what he says and thus what he does.

The sheep and goats were separated by what they did or didn't do. This is how it goes. I was thirsty; you, sheep, gave Me drink. I was hungry; you, sheep, gave Me food. I was naked; you, sheep, clothed Me; etc. You, sheep (those who "did" these things), enter into the Father's rest. You, goats (you who "did nothing"), outer darkness for you.

What did Jesus really teach? What was He doing? Jesus was bringing to us a "life change." I have always said that the Bible is more than believable; it is livable. Jesus did not come to simply start a new religion or a new movement, not even a new creed or set of doctrines. He came to the earth to change our lives, to literally transform us and cause a metamorphosis.

Jesus' entire message was a message of life—eternal life for eternal death, healing for sickness, deliverance from evil, liberty from bondage, holiness for worldliness, righteousness and peace before God. It was never Jesus' intention to give you eternal life while leaving you a servant of sin and satan. Once you meet Jesus, you will begin to change from the inside out.

One of Jesus' most significant characteristic acts is to change things. He is an expert at it. His very first miracle was to change water into wine (Jn. 2:1-11). New wine is freshly squeezed from the vine, the purest form of the grape's juice. It's called the "best" wine. Modern man (including many churchgoers) seem to mistakenly believe that the word "wine" in this text describing Christ's first miracle is talking about fermented wine with alcohol. They seem to like this "juice" better than the pure fruit of the vine. When Jesus turned the water into wine, it wasn't better because it contained more alcohol than the juice earlier served. It was better because it was the freshest, best non-alcoholic beverage they had sipped all day. (I know, all the winebibbers are now agitated with me.)

Jesus is still doing this today. Once you are born again, you are miraculously changed. You become a new vessel, capable of receiving the "new wine," the Holy Spirit (Matt. 9:17). The Lord will take all your old "fermented" things (a process of something dying) and the broken-down areas of your life and change them and make them new again.

Jesus' message was clear—the same message that John the Baptist preached: the Kingdom of God. Jesus preached repentance. He preached deliverance. He preached and taught warning after warning about the way you talk and walk, friendships, relationships, heart conditions, and more. In other words, He taught us that with His anointing and His Word, we can and should live a different life. No more sin, sickness, and spirit of the world. Transformed from darkness to His glorious light.

Jesus administered the power of forgiveness but not without confrontation and confession. He taught eternal life but only to those who believed. He called us to follow Him but not the way we want to—the way He says to. Remember the rich young ruler? Read and learn. What about the story of the servant turned over to the tormentors for unforgiveness and holding a grudge against another brother? What about Martha and Mary and the lesson learned by them to balance being a student with being a servant?

Jesus is in our life today, and He still believes what He preached as the teacher from the seashores of Galilee. His message is clear, and so are His goals—and that includes His goals for your life.

Jesus' message is good news, but it is best enjoyed by those who change to right living and turn from the old way of life. We are to deny ourselves and leave our way of life and adapt to His. We are to come out from among them and be separate, says the Lord.

Be watchful to whom you listen and even who is feeding you the gospel. Pray for your preacher that he will be a straight shooter and deal with the Word with the fear of God and no fear of man. There are many modern-day speakers who are preaching a self-seeking, self-promoting gospel. There are a lot of "benefits only" oriented preachers as well. Pray for your preacher that he will be bold and re-preach the messages of Jesus Christ as his main course.

Barclay Proverb: "You cannot serve God any way you want to; you must serve Him the way He says to in His Word."

3

Do We Preach the Full Gospel?

Are our preachers ashamed of Jesus' ministry? I know this is a strange question but one that needs to be asked.

It seems as though some are partially ashamed of Jesus' lifestyle and His message. I will admit that as I travel across our great country of America and stand among the churches, I find a message being preached that doesn't sound like Jesus Christ. As I said in the last chapter, even modern-day preachers should echo Jesus Christ.

We work for Jesus, and we should be emphasizing His truth and messages. Sure, we are to preach and teach the whole Bible. A good minister of the Word is going to take you from cover to cover, from Genesis to Revelation. A good Bible student will read and study the entire Bible. The Bible is the complete text or collection of the Scriptures, preserved for us by the holy saints before us. We are to know the Scriptures and commit to memory as many as we possibly can, for the heart of God is found in them.

What is the full gospel? It is the entire package of Jesus Christ. Nothing left out. Nothing at all. It is both the popular and the unpopular. It is His entire message—His promises and His challenges. It is His entire take on life. A full-gospel preacher or teacher is one who teaches it all. He is not a specialist in just one area. He doesn't concentrate on just one set of truths. His followers are well grounded in the Book, and they believe and have received the whole package.

What is the whole package? Everything I just mentioned. It is a lifetime spent chasing God and enjoying every experience in Him. It is being born again, water baptized, and filled with the Holy Spirit. It is speaking in tongues. It is clinging to His promises and standing on them. It is purging yourself and washing yourself with the water of the Word of God.

The Word is working whether I work it or not. IT will work for me or against me.

It is not full gospel to cling to only partial truths or receive only part of the provision. It is not full gospel to preach or believe your favorite parts of the Bible and leave out the rest. All of us who are Bible students must stick to the whole message. Be careful not to get oblong. If you study a topic or subject more often or more thoroughly than others, you tend to lean toward it most often. This will cause you to always want to study, read, and talk about that topic or subject more than others. If you are a teacher or preacher, you will want to preach about it most. Before you know it, you will feel like an expert in that area.

I realize that each of us has a strength and certain things about which we are most convicted. All of us must guard that we stay full gospel and not specialized or segregated to one set of truths. The Good Shepherd taught all truths. He was a well-balanced individual and taught the whole Kingdom. He presented the whole gospel for the whole man to everyone who heard Him. It included salvation, healing, deliverance, life, light, conviction, confrontation, a call to repentance, and more—much more.

Jesus was and is our Passover Lamb. We must not pick and choose to eat only the part that we enjoy the most—you know, our favorites. We must eat the whole lamb. When the original Passover took place, God instructed His people to eat the whole lamb and place the blood on the doorpost. When the spirit of death came to that neighborhood, it would pass them by. I believe many Christians today are still suffering and living below Christ's provisions because they do not accept the whole lamb.

do not read all the Word and meditate upon it.

They pick and choose to follow after only the parts they like, the ones they enjoy.

Just because *you* do not "believe" or "endorse" something in the Word doesn't mean it isn't true. Barclay Proverb: "Your endorsement of the Bible adds no credibility to it and doesn't make it any more true, and your lack of endorsement takes no credibility from it and makes it no less the truth." The truth is the truth, and it is established in Heaven forever.

Let's get back to the opening question of this chapter. Are preachers ashamed of any part of Jesus' ministry? Are believers ashamed of certain truths or requirements of Christ? Do we neglect certain parts of the lifestyle of Christians because we do not want our friends or neighbors to label us accordingly? Do we cheat in our worship services because we are ashamed of some of the forms of expression and believe it chases away visitors? Are we user-friendly, or Jesus-friendly? Was Jesus friendly?

I am for reaching visitors, but not at all costs. Sure, I want to evangelize. Yes, I realize there is no task any closer to the heart of God than winning souls. But I also realize we cannot pollute the Scriptures and become sacrilegious. We must protect the things that are holy to keep them holy, and the same for the sacred things.

Sacrilege is an intentional injury to anything sacred or held sacred, or the disrespectful treatment of anyone or anything sacred. Isn't it foolish to try to use the form of godliness to attract people to God if we are doing it with sacrilege?

It is ridiculous to be ashamed of God and His Holy Spirit and then try to invite people to meet Him. You can't kick out the Holy Spirit from your meetings and then invite people to meet Him. If you do, they aren't going to meet *Him*; they are going to meet *us*. They aren't really going to be introduced to the ways of Almighty God; they are going to be introduced to our ways.

Jesus was a corrector. Are you, preacher? Is your pastor one who corrects the wrong and makes straight the crooked paths? We all know that a constant diet of correction and rebuke is unhealthy (or at least unbalanced), but not any more so than a diet that totally lacks correction and rebuke. There are reasons for correction. The Word was meant to correct us when we are contrary to it.

2 TIMOTHY 3:16-17

All scripture is given by inspiration of God, and is profitable for doctrine, for reproof, for correction, for instruction in righteousness: That the man of God may be perfect, thoroughly furnished unto all good works.

The great Apostle Paul, in his instructions to Pastor Timothy, included the directives to reprove, rebuke, and correct the believers. The Amplified Bible reveals that pastors are to show people in what way their lives are wrong. Here's a verse for you:

2 TIMOTHY 4:1-2 AMP

I charge [you] in the presence of God and of Christ Jesus, Who is to judge the living and the dead, and by (in the light of) His coming and His kingdom: Herald *and* preach the Word! Keep your sense of urgency [stand by, be at hand and ready], whether the opportunity seems to be favorable or unfavorable. [Whether it is convenient or inconvenient, whether it is welcome or unwelcome, you as preacher of the Word are to show people in what way their lives are wrong.] And convince them, rebuking *and* correcting, warning *and* urging *and* encouraging them, being unflagging *and* inexhaustible in patience and teaching.

Jesus was a confronter. He didn't confront every little thing that was out of order. He did, however, confront when He knew it would spare someone great pain or fix them if they were broken. It seems like preachers today are afraid of this or fear its outcome. Jesus confronted many things and many people. I think of Peter, whom He called satan. What about the woman at the well? Or what about the warning to deny the leaven of the Pharisees when they were actually present?

The full gospel includes all the provisions of Christ and the benefits of His sacrifice. This includes healing, peace, happiness, salvation, prosperity, and more. The red letters teach us over and again to live right in the eyes of the Lord. You can't even read a chapter or two of Jesus' teaching without this valuable truth confronting you. Much of Jesus' teaching was about living the new life—from old wineskins to new ones, from the tainted cloth to the scarlet one (Matt. 9:16-17). He came to forgive us and change us forever.

The system of repentance and seeking forgiveness is not just for the sinner. It is also for the child of God (1 Jn. 1:9). We must be ready to repent. We must be ready to confess (own up to and admit) our sins. We must turn from our ways and be a follower of Jesus and not a rich young ruler (Lk. 18:18-25). A good pastor will preach repentance and forgiveness to his church members, knowing that many of them are in active sin. The truth will set you free.

A good shepherd teaches his flock all the warnings of Christ. Most of Jesus' teaching was for the day in which we now live. He constantly made reference to the last days and to the day of His coming. A good shepherd also teaches his flock about these last-days warnings—not to keep everyone dwelling on the negative or to be constantly sin-conscious but teaching the last-days warnings as a *warning*. If we are warned, we can prepare. Remember, Paul told Pastor Timothy to watch and pray so we can be counted worthy to escape all these things that will come down upon the earth.

Okay, so what if we *don't* do this?

A good shepherd echoes Jesus Christ and not just his modern hero. He patterns his life and teaching material after Jesus, the Christ, and not a contemporary. I'm telling you straight that we have lost much of this in the local church. We must be found teaching the parables of Jesus, and the flock must read these red letters often—more than any other text.

Are we sheep, or pigs? The Apostle Peter referred to some church members as "sows" (2 Pet. 2:22). Jesus' teaching refers many times to shepherds and sheep. We must follow as sheep and stay in the fold and never again look to the world to go back to it. We are not dogs returning to what we have vomited. There is a big difference between washed and dirty. Everyone knows this, but they seem to want to apply it to the body only. However, your soul can be soiled, and your spiritual life dirtied.

Look at 2 Corinthians 7:1 with me:

2 CORINTHIANS 7:1

> Having therefore these promises, dearly beloved, let us cleanse ourselves from all filthiness of the flesh and spirit, perfecting holiness in the fear of God.

It is also interesting that some people think we were washed once and never need anything again. This is an extreme exaggeration of the provision of salvation. I am not of the school that we can lose our salvation every time we sin, but I am also not of the school that we should behave like rich young rulers who meet Jesus and then turn away but somehow believe we are still close to Him and okay with Him.

REVELATION 3:4-5

> Thou hast a few names even in Sardis which have not defiled their garments; and they shall walk with me in white: for they are worthy. He that overcometh, the same shall be clothed in white raiment; and I will not blot out his name out of the book of life, but I will confess his name before my Father, and before his angels.

4

The Words of Life

MATTHEW 24:35

> Heaven and earth shall pass away, but my words shall not
> pass away.

WHERE WOULD WE GO?

JOHN 6:68

> Then Simon Peter answered him, Lord, to whom shall
> we go? thou hast the words of eternal life.

Everyone who ever met Jesus Christ has this same take on things.
In fact, I would seriously question anyone's salvation encounter
with Christ if they feel differently. We all have been changed
forever and ever. We all know where life comes from. We all
know it is His Word in us that has totally transformed our lives.

We did not just "get religion" or join a moral Bible-reading club.
We did not pick up a new habit. You know, there's golfing,
hunting, fishing, and church membership. No! We have been
changed inside forever. We are born again; and we were once
dead to sin, but now we are alive in Him.

Here is the power of Christ and the Word: "To open their eyes,
and to turn them from darkness to light, and from the power of

satan unto God, that they may receive forgiveness of sins, and inheritance among them which are sanctified by faith that is in me" (Acts 26:18).

I hear people say all the time that they are going to quit. I guess they mean quit the church, the Bible, and God. But where will they go? To turn away from church is to go to the world. To turn away from the Bible is to turn to philosophy and psychology. To turn away from the Spirit of Christ is to turn to familiar spirits and witchcraft—from light to dark, from love and peace to anger and hatred, and so on.

WHY THE RED LETTERS?

JOHN 6:63 NKJV

> It is the Spirit who gives life; the flesh profits nothing. The words that I speak to you are spirit, and they are life.

Why the red letters? Because they are spirit, and they are life—that's why. The entrance of these Words of Christ not only brings knowledge and understanding to the mind but light to the soul. These words bring to us the heart of Christ and His teachings, and they insert into us His opinion, attitude, and Spirit. The absence of these red letters eliminates all the above.

We need to know more about Jesus, our Savior, than any other person in the Bible. We need to know more about His actual teachings and parables than any other truths anywhere.

Our society is slowly turning Jesus from our Lord and Savior to just a religious figure, and from God Almighty Himself to a prophet and teacher. This is a tragedy.

1 JOHN 5:12 NKJV

> He who has the Son has life; he who does not have the Son of God does not have life.

". . . thou hast the words of eternal life" (Jn. 6:68). Many times throughout my life I have run to the red letters in my Bible.

There I found comfort, healing, encouragement, and direction. They have never failed me.

I have witnessed that many people discourage themselves simply by what they read or what they say. You can read things that bring you down, and you can read things that bring you up. I have never understood why so many people run to things that hurt them when they are already hurting. They run to false doctrines, false prophets, entertainers, psychics, and even drugs and booze. There is no life in these things.

There is life in the Word! There is life for your marriage. There is life for your body. There is life for your children. There is physical life and healing. There is inner healing and life. There is spiritual life. There is hope, and there is encouragement.

You should have a Bible and mark certain verses that mean something special to you so when you are in trouble or in severe warfare, you don't have to take the time to research. It is good to read any scripture, but the ones that mean something special to you will minister to you in a greater way. I love the Bible. It has always enhanced my life. It has always brought strength to me. It has always built me up and given me the inner fortitude to move forward.

For many years I have heard people say, "What would Jesus do?" I like that, actually. We should ask ourselves this question every time we are about to make a major decision. In fact, we should think about what Jesus would do every time we do anything. Our entire life should be patterned after Jesus, our Christ, and everything we do should bring Him glory and represent Him well.

The only accurate place to see what Jesus would do is in the red letters of your Bible. It is the place in your Bible where you can see the truthful, biblical portrait of Jesus and how He handled everything and everyone.

5

The Delivering Red Letters

The red letters promise us deliverance from the wicked one and from ourselves. In fact, the greatest promises for freedom are in the Words of Christ.

MATTHEW 1:21

> And she shall bring forth a son, and thou shalt call his name JESUS: for he shall save his people from their sins.

This verse really says it all. Jesus had a purpose in coming to the earth. It was for you. It was for me. It was to separate us from the terrible pain and destruction of sin. It was to deliver us from the sinful nature itself. I have watched people cling to that old nature with all that is within them, as if they would die if they let it go. As a pastor of many years, I have witnessed people destroy all or parts of their life by allowing the practice of sin. They have destroyed their health, family, marriage, money, reputation, and much more. But I have seen great liberty and freedom come to those who beat sin, once and for all.

To be delivered from sin is to be delivered from the old sinful nature. You can easily say that to be delivered from the sinful nature is to be delivered from yourself. That's right, Jesus came to deliver you from yourself. He came to deliver you from being your own Lord, calling your own shots, and the power of your own flesh. We can apply this verse in our lives even more deeply. To be separated from the old sinful, fallen nature and become a partaker of His divine nature is what it's all about.

I know this because I am a delivered man myself. After I got born again and began to study the Bible, I found deliverance from my old self and from my former habits. It was awesome to see how fast God delivered me, and how fast I learned the way of the Kingdom.

2 PETER 1:4

> Whereby are given unto us exceeding great and precious promises: that by these ye might be partakers of the divine nature, having escaped the corruption that is in the world through lust.

ACTS 26:18

> To open their eyes, and to turn them from darkness to light, and from the power of Satan unto God, that they may receive forgiveness of sins, and inheritance among them which are sanctified by faith that is in me.

TITUS 2:11-12

> For the grace of God that bringeth salvation hath appeared to all men, Teaching us that, denying ungodliness and worldly lusts, we should live soberly, righteously, and godly, in this present world . . .

JOHN 6:68

> Then Simon Peter answered him, Lord, to whom shall we *go*? thou hast the words of eternal life.

JOHN 5:14

> Afterward Jesus findeth him in the temple, and said unto him, Behold, thou art made whole: sin no more, lest a worse thing come unto thee.

JOHN 8:11

She said, No man, Lord. And Jesus said unto her,
Neither do I condemn thee: go, and sin no more.

Please let Him do it! Allow Him the access to that old nature through total surrender to Him and His Word. Once you do this without reservation, you will enter a new conquering lifestyle as well as a higher quality of life.

JOHN 8:36

If the Son therefore shall make you free, ye shall be
free indeed.

This is awesome! It tells us that it's for real. It's not a false promise. It's not just getting your hopes up and then a terrible letdown. It is the provision of Christ. It is ours.

Freedom—there is nothing like it. We are no longer a prisoner or hostage to the flesh and its demanding and belittling abuses. We are to be free—free to live without sin in our life, free to break the bands of wickedness and to undo the heavy burdens. Thank God we didn't just get religion, but we got born again. Old things have passed away; and behold, all things have become new.

Religion is a swap. It is swapping your old music for new music. It is swapping your old hangout place for a new one. Religion is just a list of do's and don'ts but with no power to do the do's or to stop doing the don'ts. We did not just get religion. We are born again and converted by the precious Word of God. We are changed from the inside out, and we are now chasing Him and His lifestyle.

1 PETER 1:23

Being born again, not of corruptible seed, but of
incorruptible, by the word of God, which liveth and
abideth for ever.

I am a living epistle of this very thing, once a bound sinner but now free. I pray for you that you continue your journey as a follower of Jesus Christ. May you overcome all obstacles, including your own old nature, and may you conquer life.

JOHN 5:14

Afterward Jesus findeth him in the temple, and said unto him, Behold, thou art made whole: ~~sin no more~~, lest a worse thing come unto thee.

JOHN 8:11

She said, No man, Lord. And Jesus said unto her, Neither do I condemn thee: go, and ~~sin no more~~.

Live—and live sin free!

6

The Healing Red Letters

JESUS HEALED AND DELIVERED

LUKE 4:40-41

Now when the sun was setting, all they that had any sick with divers diseases brought them unto him; and he laid his hands on every one of them, and healed them. And devils also came out of many, crying out, and saying, Thou art Christ the Son of God. And he rebuking them suffered them not to speak: for they knew that he was Christ.

ROOF OFF—BED DOWN—MAN HEALED

MARK 2:1-5

And again he entered into Capernaum after some days; and it was noised that he was in the house. And straightway many were gathered together, insomuch that there was no room to receive them, no, not so much as about the door: and he preached the word unto them. And they come unto him, bringing one sick of the palsy, which was borne of four. And when they could not come nigh unto him for the press, they uncovered the roof where he was: and when they had broken it up, they let down the bed wherein the sick of the palsy lay. When

Jesus saw their faith, he said unto the sick of the palsy, <u>Son, thy sins be forgiven thee</u>.

MARK 2:12

And immediately he arose, took up the bed, and went forth before them all; insomuch that they were all amazed, and glorified God, saying, We never saw it on this fashion.

JESUS HEALED THEM ALL

LUKE 6:19

And the whole multitude sought to touch him: for there went virtue out of him, and healed them all.

LUKE 4:40

Now when the sun was setting, all they that had any sick with divers diseases brought them unto him; and he laid his hands on every one of them, and healed them.

THE WORD GREW MIGHTILY—PREVAILED

ACTS 19:18-20

And many that believed came, and confessed, and shewed their deeds. Many of them also which used curious arts brought their books together, and burned them before all men: and they counted the price of them, and found it fifty thousand pieces of silver. So mightily grew the word of God and prevailed.

PERSONAL TESTIMONIES

I will never forget the day our doctor broke the news to us that Vickie had cancer, and it was aggressive and invasive. Even though we are faith people, it immediately hit us in the center of our belly. I will also always remember what Vickie told the doctor that day, "We don't just preach the gospel, Doc. We live it. You do what you do, and Jesus will do what He does, and I will get a miracle."

When we left the office that day, we sat awhile in the car.
The first thing that came to me was how to fight this enemy.
I remembered what I was trained to do in the Marines in
Vietnam when fear came upon us. FACE IT—HEAD ON!
So Vickie and I talked about the best that could happen and the
worst that could happen. When we were done discussing the
worst-case scenario, a great strength came to us. We realized
that facing even death only presents a great opportunity for a
Christian to achieve the greatest of all victories. After all,
Heaven is the ultimate goal.

Our battle wasn't over that day, but the fear was gone. We
downgraded it to a lesser enemy. About 32 days after this date, we
went back to the doctor's office. It was so powerful to have him
say, "You are totally free from cancer." What a great day that was!

If you want to read more of this powerful testimony, get Vickie's
daily devotional, *One Day–One Thought–One Year*, or you can
get her testimony audio recording and *hear* her tell the story. It is
powerful. It has helped many people because Jesus still heals today.

I remember one day in our church in Midland, Michigan, when
the Holy Spirit gave me a word of knowledge (a gift of the Spirit,
1 Cor. 12:7-9). The Lord said to me, "There is a man here with
severe stomach issues." I called out the man the Lord pointed out
to me. I prophesied over him that the Lord was going to help
him in his struggles and deliver him from the snare of the enemy.
It was about two weeks later that he contacted me and said he
was healed from cancer in his stomach and had undergone a
battery of tests so he would have the proof from the doctors.
Jesus still heals today.

Many years ago there was a Baptist preacher in our town who
had issues with my "kind of ministry," as he put it. One day,
however, he accepted the challenge of a loved one to come to one
of my meetings. I had never met him before, neither did I know
he had any issues with me. In that meeting the Lord spoke to me
to call out a particular man who didn't believe the Lord healed
today, and the Lord was going to prove the man wrong. So I did

exactly as the Lord instructed me. The man was reluctant and seemed very nervous but came forward as I requested. I prayed over him. In an instant, he shouted and began to shake a leg and then jump a little. When I asked him what was happening, he said, "I believe I am healed." His damaged leg of many years was completely made whole. It was that same Baptist minister. Jesus still heals today.

I was preaching at a convention on the Eastern Seaboard, and in the middle of the meeting God spoke to me to call out a lady in front of me. As she came forward, I received a word of knowledge about her health and that the Lord was going to speed up her metabolism and rush healing power through her blood. She was very heavy and looked very tired and sickly. It was a few weeks later when she contacted our office and sent a photo. Vickie and I were both overwhelmed and overjoyed. She had lost so much weight. In a few more weeks she contacted us again. Her story was so impressive that we had her come to the church to testify. When she stood on our platform, she held up a shirt she had worn the day I called her out weeks before. It covered both her and me, with some left over. Wow! One word from Heaven, and the Jesus of Matthew, Mark, Luke, and John sped up her metabolism, and she lost many, many pounds.

There are so many testimonies of His healing power. In all our years of ministry, He has always shown up and confirmed the Word we preach with signs following. He still heals today.

The Darkest, Brightest Day of Our Life

It was a beautiful Saturday at my home in Michigan. We had just celebrated my grandson Dakota's graduation. Most guests and family members had gone home. My daughter Dawn, her husband James, their children, and a few friends decided to swim a while. As they were enjoying the day, my ten-year-old granddaughter Jadyn got caught in the suction of the poolside vent. As her long hair bundled up in the tube, she couldn't pull herself away. She soon became unconscious and drowned.

One of her little girlfriends who was swimming with her told her daddy (my son-in-law James) that Jadyn was not coming up.

She was underwater about three minutes. It took all of James' strength to pull her away from the pool suction and get her up on the deck. He and a friend started CPR immediately but were tempted to lose hope after almost two minutes went by. No pulse, no heartbeat, no visible life. My daughter and a friend were yelling out their faith. "In Jesus' name, you will live and not die! Help us, Jesus! We rebuke death, in Jesus' name!"

Vickie and I were in another city; and when my daughter called me, we immediately went to war with them. Vickie began to call out to Jesus to spare her life. "Jesus, don't let her die! Jesus, I call upon You now, that in Your name she will come back to life!" I began to claim tither's rights. "Lord, we are all tithers. Vickie and I have tithed since the first sermon we ever heard on the subject. We claim tither's rights, right now, in Jesus' name! Lord, You said that as we tithe, You will rebuke the devourer on our behalf. I call upon You, Lord God, to rebuke death, right now, in Jesus' name!" Then I felt this surge come up out of my innermost being, and I began to yell out loud, "Not today, satan. Not today, death. The Lord rebuke you. The Lord is about to swat you severely because we are tithers, and you *will* be rebuked!"

All of a sudden Jadyn shook and came alive. She began to yell out, and life reentered her little body. She was no longer cold to the touch. Her eyes opened. We all began to rejoice and thank the Lord for His mercy and grace. I began to thank God for His promises to the tither.

First a local hospital and then a children's trauma center unit reported there was no damage to Jadyn's body or her brain. None whatsoever. She was released in less than 24 hours with a perfect bill of health. The medical experts kept telling us that we had experienced an absolute miracle. They kept telling us that there should be issues with anyone who was out that long.

We will never forget the spirit of death that overshadowed us that day, but we will also never stop rejoicing that although it was one of our darkest days, because of Jesus keeping His Word with the tither, it is one of our brightest days. Thank You, Jesus!

YOU SEEK HIM FOR IT

The Woman With the Issue of Blood

MARK 5:24-34

- She was sick 12 years.
- She spent all she had on doctors.
- She said within herself . . .
- She risked the danger of being found in public with a forbidden and punishable issue of blood.
- She pressed into the crowd.
- She touched the hem of His garment.
- She used every bit of faith she had.
- She was healed completely.

YOU CRY OUT TO HIM FOR IT

Blind Bartimaeus

MARK 10:46-52

- He was born blind.
- He heard that Jesus was passing his way.
- He went to where Jesus was.
- He cried out louder than all.
- When told to shut up, he cried out even louder.
- He was miraculously healed.

There are so many more great healing stories in the red letters of our New Testament. Read them all, and rejoice. If you are battling sickness and disease, please do not give up. Keep crying out to God like blind Bartimaeus. Press in even harder to touch the hem of His garment. If you contact Vickie and me, we will stand with you for your healing, and we will pray over you, in Jesus' name.

HEBREWS 13:8

Jesus Christ the same yesterday, and to day, and for ever.

7

Red Letters That Take You to Heaven

I want to remind you once again that I recommend reading the entire Bible from cover to cover. Every Word of God is inspired by God and profitable to your life (2 Tim. 3:16). In this book, *The Missing Red Letters*, I am simply trying to bring to your attention the great importance of the teachings of Jesus Christ while He walked this earth.

There is no doubt that these Words of Christ are enough to take you to Heaven. All we have to do is read them, believe them, and apply them to our life. In other words, know what Jesus Christ taught, and obey His teachings. A great apostle once said you should kneel down and read the four gospels straight through three times so the anointing of Christ will come upon you. That was Dr. Oral Roberts.

I realize the ultimate goal is to make Heaven, escape eternal damnation, and enjoy eternal salvation. However, I know there are other great benefits to our walk with God. For example, even while we are on this earth we can live in victory, health, peace, and prosperity.

The elements of this world, the works of the flesh, and the deception of satan are all enemies of your life. By following the red letters in your Bible, you will have both the information as well as the power to beat these enemies. To become a victor, a conqueror, and to master this life, we must submit to Jesus and His way of life. It is a part of our covenant and what the Lord Jesus expects of us.

I decided many years ago that I was on my way to Heaven. I read in these great red letters that the way to Heaven is straight and narrow, and only few find it. There are only two highways to life (or life after death)—this straight and narrow way to Heaven, and the wide road to hell.

MATTHEW 7:13-14

> Enter ye in at the strait gate: for wide is the gate, and broad is the way, that leadeth to destruction, and many there be which go in thereat: Because strait is the gate, and narrow is the way, which leadeth unto life, and few there be that find it.

I certainly was on my way to hell. Once I made up my mind to go to Heaven, I have fought every element in this life that would hold me back. I have severed every connection to every element that could weaken me, draw me away from the Words of Christ, and lead me to hell.

Most of the preaching in these last days eliminates any explanation or definition of eternal damnation. But eternity is eternity. Therefore eternal damnation lasts as long as eternal salvation. There are many different ideas about life after death. Since no one really knows, I have chosen to listen to Jesus Christ and take His recommendations. I advise you to do exactly the same thing, without exception and without flaw.

When I gave my life to Jesus Christ and invited Him to live in my heart, asking Him to forgive me and cleanse me from all unrighteousness, it was the first time in my entire life that I "felt alive." It was my heart—not a book, a friend, or something I had heard once before—that instructed me to find the house of God and become a part of the army of God.

When I first began searching for a church and to become a part of God's people, I had no idea what to look for. I was never raised in church. However, I did know what I wasn't looking for, and that was somebody like me. Thank God, the church I found was not filled with smokers, drinkers, or those who cuss and carouse. I was looking for people who had given up all this and who walked with God—genuine Christians, blood-washed and meaning business with God. I am free from all vices today because I was surrounded by true, delivered, practicing Christians and not fake or carnal ones.

I have great advice for all you contemporary churches, pastors, and believers. Stop trying to act and look like a sinner to attract sinners. This really does not work in the end. In fact, it normally backfires. I have seen more good, hungry Christians grow cool and become worldly by watering down things and lowering the standard to attract the sinner. Once again, I remind you that sinners and new converts are not only unashamed of Christ but are actually looking for the real deal. We cannot preach the world to the world to win the world. It is great to get people in the church, but what eternal good is it if they do not have an encounter with Jesus Christ and are given a placebo instead of the real thing?

JOHN 5:39

Search the scriptures; for in them ye think ye have eternal life: and they are they which testify of me.

MATTHEW 25:46

And these shall go away into everlasting punishment: but the righteous into life eternal.

JOHN 3:15

That whosoever believeth in him should not perish, but have eternal life.

JOHN 3:16

For God so loved the world, that he gave his only begotten Son, that whosoever believeth in him should not perish, but have everlasting life.

JOHN 4:36

And he that reapeth receiveth wages, and gathereth fruit unto life eternal: that both he that soweth and he that reapeth may rejoice together.

JOHN 10:28

And I give unto them eternal life; and they shall never perish, neither shall any *man* pluck them out of my hand.

JOHN 17:2

As thou hast given him power over all flesh, that he should give eternal life to as many as thou hast given him.

JOHN 17:3

And this is life eternal, that they might know thee the only true God, and Jesus Christ, whom thou hast sent.

REVELATION 3:5

He that overcometh, the same shall be clothed in white raiment; and I will not blot out his name out of the book of life, but I will confess his name before my Father, and before his angels.

8

Warning Red Letters

FALSE DOCTRINES—FALSE PROPHETS

As you read through the teachings of Jesus Christ, you discover that He was constantly warning us about the dangers of things to come. When I say things to come, I am referring to things that would happen from the time of Christ forward—that is to say, *our* day. It seems that most of the parables and many of the teachings of Jesus were pointed, to some degree, to the day in which you and I now live. There is no doubt He was trying to warn us of the false spiritual things.

For example, the verses I have listed below are from the Gospel of Matthew. It is clear that these false spiritual things are listed here by Jesus on purpose. Do not be fooled to think that everything labeled church and religion, or anyone labeled reverend, bishop, or pastor is of God and pure in motive or lifestyle. It should bother you as much as it bothers me to know that Jesus tells of "many" who will be deceived by these false preachers, hiding under the cloak of true sheep. I would like to point out here that Jesus not only warns us about the whole deception problem but that "many" will be fooled—not a few, but "many."

MATTHEW 7:15

Beware of false prophets, which come to you in sheep's clothing, but inwardly they are ravening wolves.

MATTHEW 24:11

And many false prophets shall rise, and shall deceive many.

FALSE REVIVALS

Jesus also tried to warn us about false christs. Can you imagine that? Not false saviors, rather those who claim to be the Anointed One. For several years now I have watched what I call false revivals—preachers and their followers, claiming they have the anointing, presented in such a way through marketing and imaging that they seem to be the *only* ones with the anointing and their leader is the new anointed one. Many people go to these meetings to bring back this new anointing to their churches and their cities.

Don't misunderstand me, I am totally for revival, and I am personally believing for an outpouring of the great Holy Spirit throughout the land. However, I am not going to be deceived by these self-made meetings, filled with pretense, exaggerations, and false signs, wonders, and miracles. I know that many people do not understand that false ministers can do signs, wonders, and powerful things; but the truth is, they can. And they do it with a familiar spirit and the empowerment of satan. In the verse below, Jesus was very clear that even the very elect will be deceived if possible.

MATTHEW 24:24

For there shall arise false Christs, and false prophets, and shall shew great signs and wonders; insomuch that, if it were possible, they shall deceive the very elect.

MARK 13:22

For false Christs and false prophets shall rise, and shall shew signs and wonders, to seduce, if it were possible, even the elect.

We are not done witnessing these kinds of meetings or these false preachers. More and more, we will see a desperate satan working with seducing and familiar spirits to fool mankind, with the goal to ultimately draw all of us away from the truth and into error, away from the true Christ into these counterfeit spiritual parties.

FALSE SHEPHERDS & HIRELINGS

In the Gospel of John, we find that Jesus warned us about shepherds who do not really care for the sheep. In other words, they are more concerned about their job, their money, and their own prosperity than the condition of the sheep. He reveals that the false shepherd leaves when the going gets tough and the attack from the enemy is prevailing. This kind of preacher leaves when the money is down and their personal comfort and benefit is threatened. They abandon their care of that flock and go on to other fields of supply.

I realize this sounds a little tough, and I'm taking the risk of some people thinking I'm just being critical or unfair. Not so. I am referring to the same thing to which Jesus referred.

Read this passage:

JOHN 10:12-13

> But he that is an hireling, and not the shepherd, whose own the sheep are not, seeth the wolf coming, and leaveth the sheep, and fleeth: and the wolf catcheth them, and scattereth the sheep. The hireling fleeth, because he is an hireling, and careth not for the sheep.

SIN

I could write volumes today on the terrible pain and destruction that sin has on a human's life. I have been a leader in this Kingdom for many years now. I am now considered an elder and father in the faith over many believers and even a multitude of ministers. No matter who you are or what you are, no one is exempt from the penalties of sin.

It is not God who wants to judge you or punish you. Quite the contrary, He sent His only begotten Son to save you and cleanse you from all unrighteousness. However, I seem to be living in a day when even God's children want to fight for their right to be carnal, filthy, worldly, and unscriptural. In all my years as a Christian and a Christian leader, I have never seen such a fervent attempt to mix the world with the Church.

Haven't you heard this? "Sin will take you further than you wanted to go, keep you longer than you wanted to stay, and cost you more than you ever intended to pay."

The Book of Job (and most of the Bible) teaches us that our sin and wrongdoings will root out all our increase (Job 31:12). My advice to you (or better yet, Christ's advice to you) is to stay out of sin. Fight it with everything that is within you. It reminds me of the words of the angel sent to Joseph:

MATTHEW 1:21

> And she shall bring forth a son, and thou shalt call his name JESUS: for he shall save his people from their sins.

JOHN 5:14

> Afterward Jesus findeth him in the temple, and said unto him, Behold, thou art made whole: sin no more, lest a worse thing come unto thee.

JOHN 8:11

> She said, No man, Lord. And Jesus said unto her, Neither do I condemn thee: go, and sin no more.

JOHN 8:34

> Jesus answered them, Verily, verily, I say unto you, Whosoever committeth sin is the servant of sin.

JOHN 16:8-11

> And when he is come, he will reprove the world of sin,
> and of righteousness, and of judgment: Of sin, because
> they believe not on me; Of righteousness, because I go
> to my Father, and ye see me no more; Of judgment,
> because the prince of this world is judged.

MAN GETS HIS WAY

Finally, it seems that man gets his way, even with the gospel. In
today's newest movement, the goal is to attract people at all costs.
In fact, that is what the money is spent on. No matter what it
takes, let's get people in the doors of our church. Man has always
wanted to live his life the way he thinks is good. And man has
always wanted to escape damnation and hell in some way without
being "put out" by serving God. Man has always wanted to
appease his conscience through religion and sort of pretend he is
right in God's sight. "There is a way which seemeth right unto a
man, but the end thereof are the ways of death" (Prov. 14:12).

Beware of church in the flesh. That's right, church in the flesh.
We now live in the time where churches are capitalizing on
carnality. Many preachers are attracting a multitude of people
who want to serve God the way they want to and live filthy but
claim they are righteous. Many pulpits in America are now filled
with sinners and those who actually lead God's people into a
form of permission to sin. Many claim this is grace. But over
and again, the teachings of Jesus Christ and the great apostles of
the New Testament have always taught a grace message totally
contrary to this.

I do not say these things to be abrasive or even corrective to those
who do it. I say these things to simply stand with Jesus and
warn you to separate yourself from sin as fast as you possibly can.
Take the warning of Jesus Christ, and go and sin no more, lest
something worse happens to you.

JOHN 5:14

> Afterward Jesus findeth him in the temple, and said unto him, Behold, thou art made whole: sin no more, lest a worse thing come unto thee.

Do not go and sin *more* because you have met grace, rather sin *no* more, lest something worse happens to you!

As I awoke one morning, the Lord spoke to me and said, "I have a problem." I answered Him with, "What could be *Your* problem, Your Majesty?" He answered with, "There are multitudes of speakers in My holy desks [pulpits] who are literally teaching My people how to sear their own conscience as with a hot iron [1 Tim. 4:2]. They are teaching My people to live contrary to My lifestyle and feel no conviction about any of it."

You run from these, and turn your ears away from them and not away from the truth.

9

Red Letters in Parables

JESUS, WHY DO YOU TEACH IN PARABLES?

MATTHEW 13:10

> And the disciples came, and said unto him, Why speakest thou unto them in parables?

MATTHEW 13:11-14

> **He answered and said unto them,** Because it is given unto you to know the mysteries of the kingdom of heaven, but to them it is not given. For whosoever hath, to him shall be given, and he shall have more abundance: but whosoever hath not, from him shall be taken away even that he hath. Therefore speak I to them in parables: because they seeing see not; and hearing they hear not, neither do they understand. And in them is fulfilled the prophecy of Esaias, which saith, By hearing ye shall hear, and shall not understand; and seeing ye shall see, and shall not perceive . . .

In other words, it is a great privilege to hear and know the truth. Never take it for granted, and always be humble and appreciate the truth when it is presented to you. Many, many people will have the gospel presented to them but never understand it.

MARK 4:1-3

And he began again to teach by the sea side: and there was gathered unto him a great multitude, so that he entered into a ship, and sat in the sea; and the whole multitude was by the sea on the land. And he taught them many things by parables, and said unto them in his doctrine, Hearken; Behold, there went out a sower to sow . . .

MARK 4:10, 13

And when he was alone, they that were about him with the twelve asked of him the parable. And he said unto them, Know ye not this parable? and how then will ye know all parables?

The truth belongs to the followers of Christ. If you understand this parable, you will be able to understand all the other parables. This parable reveals to us the way the Kingdom works and how truth is released and received by us. It also reveals to us the different mindsets and heart conditions. If we understand how this works, we will be able to discern and understand the other parables because all parables are stories (vehicles) that deliver truth to the followers of Christ.

Jesus, in red letters, is showing us one of the greatest secrets of the Kingdom—a key we will have with us always, and it will unlock the parables and allegories and bring us life.

The red letters (mostly parables) are stories of everyday life, fortified supernaturally by Heaven. As followers of Christ, we listen to and read these red letters, truth is released and extracted from them, and they bring us hidden meanings, revelations, and guidance. They hold a different, deeper meaning than the normal hearer receives. They hold a secret from Heaven that God wants to disclose to His followers. Pretty awesome, huh?

I recently taught a series of messages that dealt with every parable of Christ and the hidden meanings. If you are interested in them, contact my team at *www.marktbarclay.com.*

Read and meditate on every parable of Jesus until you know the true meanings and can help other followers of Christ. Remember, many people are "mind blind." Their mind is as blind as the blind man's eyes. If I hold up a colored picture in front of a blind man, he cannot see it. It is there, and I can explain it to him explicitly; but as hard as he tries, he still cannot see it. He can only imagine.

The man with a blind mind is exactly the same. He just cannot see what you see. You can tell him all day long and even show him the Scriptures, but he won't "get it." This is why we do not debate and argue so much with sinners and backsliders. Instead, we should constantly turn the conversation back to the simple salvation messages.

Every man has been given the measure of faith—that is, enough faith to be born again when the gospel is presented. Beyond that, a new convert cannot reason intelligently with a Bible-taught, supernatural Christian.

So don't let anyone tell you to lay down your Bible. Not any part of it. That would be like surrendering your sword in the battlefield. Don't listen to any speaker who would tell you not to trust your Bible. Don't follow any minister who tells you to omit certain verses, including the Old Testament. Certainly don't allow anyone to tell you to dismiss the red letters or that these great Words of Christ are not for today. You and I were purchased by the Lord Jesus Christ. We belong to Him. We are not our own. We follow His footsteps, His style of living, His ways, and His Words. I enjoy it!

Prayer of Salvation

YOU CAN BE SAVED FROM ETERNAL DAMNATION!

Get God's help now, in this life. All you have to do is humble your heart, believe in Christ's work at Calvary for you, and pray this prayer:

Dear Heavenly Father,

I know that I have sinned and fallen short of Your expectations of me. I have come to realize that I cannot run my own life. I do not want to continue the way I've been living, neither do I want to face an eternity of torment and damnation.

I know that the wages of sin is death, but I can be spared from this through the gift of the Lord Jesus Christ. I believe that He died for me, and I receive His provision now. I will not be ashamed of Him, and I will tell all my friends and family members that I have made this wonderful decision.

Dear Lord Jesus,

Come into my heart now and live in me and be my Savior, Master, and Lord. I will do my very best to chase after You and learn Your ways by submitting to a pastor, reading my Bible, going to a church that preaches about You, and keeping sin out of my life.

I also ask You to give me the power to be healed from all sickness and disease and to deliver me from those things that have me bound.

I love You and thank You for having me, and I am eagerly looking forward to a long, beautiful relationship with You.

Amen.

Other Product by Mark Barclay Ministries

BOOKS

Avoiding the Pitfalls of Familiarity

This book is a scriptural study about the most devastating sin in the body of Christ today. The truths in this book will make you aware of this excess familiarity and reveal to you some counterattacks.

Beware of Seducing Spirits

This is not a book on demonology. It is a book about people who are close to being in trouble with God because of demonic activity or fleshly bad attitudes.

Building a Supernatural Church

A step-by-step guide to pioneering, organizing, and establishing a local church.

Enduring Hardness

God has designed a program for His saints that will cause each one to be enlarged and victorious. This book will challenge your stability, steadfastness, courage, endurance, and determination and will motivate you to become a fighter.

How to Always Reap a Harvest

In this book, Dr. Barclay explains the principles that help us to be successful and fruitful. It explains how to live a better life, become far more productive, and enjoy a full harvest.

How to Avoid Shipwreck

A book of preventives, helping people to remain strong and full of faith. You will be strengthened by this book as you learn how to anchor your soul.

How to Relate to Your Pastor

God's people all over the world are looking for ways to bless and relate to their pastor. Many want to know their responsibility to God in the way they treat him. The truths in this book will establish that right relationship with your pastor and better accomplish the gospel of the Lord Jesus Christ.

How to Survive a Betrayal

Often the most difficult thing to deal with concerning betrayal is the fact that it almost always comes from the people you love, trust, or respect. This amazing book will help you press on, recover, and once again become productive when a betrayal strikes your heart.

Improving Your Performance

Every leader everywhere needs to read this book. It will help tremendously in the organization and unity of your ministry and work force.

Man Maker—Insights on Having a Great Marriage

I was interviewed by the famous sportscaster, Mr. Pat Summerall, as one of his American Success Stories. Pat asked me for my secret to success. Without hesitation, I reported with great accuracy the passion in my heart. My answer? I had met two beings in my life who changed me forever. The first is the Lord Jesus Christ. The second is my wife Vickie. I humbly confess that without these two wonderful beings in my life, I would still be a drunk and a total loser—that is, if I were even still alive.

One Day, One Thought, One Year by Vickie Barclay

In this daily devotional for women of righteousness, Vickie has expressed her heart. It is filled with the Scriptures and God's Word. Her explanation of the Bible is precious and so needed—a tremendous way to begin each day.

Preachers of Righteousness

As you read this book, you will be both edified and challenged to not only do the work of the ministry but to do it with humility, honesty, and godliness.

Sheep, Goats, and Wolves

A scriptural yet practical explanation of human behavior in our local churches and how church leaders and members can deal with each other.

Six Ways to Check Your Leadings

It seems that staying in the main flow of Jesus is one of the most difficult things for believers to do, including some preachers. Many people border on mysticism and a world of fantasy. God is not a goofy god. He doesn't intend for His people to be goofy either. This book reveals the six most valuable New Testament ways to live in accuracy and stay perfectly on course. This book is a must for living in these last days.

The Making of a Man of God

In this book you'll find some of the greatest yet simplest insights to becoming a man or woman of God and launching your ministry with accuracy and credibility. The longevity of your ministry will be enhanced by these truths.

The Real Truth About Tithing

With the extremely fast-paced lifestyle of these last days, it leaves little time to thoroughly study God's Word. When you finish this book, you will be fully equipped and informed to tithe properly and accurately. All of your tithing questions should be answered. Your life will never be the same.

The Remnant

God has always had a people and will always have a people. Dr. Barclay speaks of the upcoming revival and how we can be those who are alive and remain when our Master returns.

The Sin of Lawlessness

Lawlessness always challenges authority and ultimately is designed to hurt people. This book will convict those who are in lawlessness and warn those who could be future victims. It will help your life and straighten your walk with Him.

Things You Need for the Day Ahead

This book was written to alert everyone (sinner and saint) to the coming perils, calamities, and filth that human power will not be able to overcome. Much of the future will be affected by holy wars and the terrible elements attached to them. This will be a prelude to the entry of the antichrist. Those who cling to truth and the Lord Jesus Christ will make it—some as survivors and some as conquerors. They will endure to the end.

Walking With God

A handbook for the Spirit-filled life, this book is sure to stir you on in pursuing more of the things of the Spirit. It also makes a great gift for those who don't understand the Spirit-filled life, giving thorough explanation, mixed with real experience, regarding the following topics: The Ministry of the Holy Spirit; The Holy Spirit in Action; No Mere Man; Holy Spirit Baptism; The Anointing; Led by the Spirit; How to Check Your Leadings; The Eyes of Your Spirit; The Armor of God; The Fruit of the Spirit; The Gifts of God; How to Develop in the Gifts; On Fire for God; Making the Holy Spirit Your Best Friend!

Warring Mental Warfare

Every person is made up of body, soul, and spirit and fights battles on each of these three fronts. The war against your soul (made up of your mind, will, and emotions) is real and as lethal as spiritual and natural enemies. This book will help you identify, war against, and defeat the enemies of your soul. Learn to quit coping with depression, anxiety, fear, and other hurts, and begin conquering those things now!

What About Death?

In this book, Brother Barclay deals with the enemy (death) and how to overcome it. He also explains what the Bible says about life after death. Many people have no real Bible knowledge on this subject and therefore are unsure about it all the days of their lives.

MINIBOOKS

Basic Christian Handbook

This book contains basic doctrines that are simple yet necessary to every Christian's walk with God. It will be a vital help to new converts in the Kingdom.

Have You Seen This Person Lately?

Did you once serve the Lord actively and fervently, but now you have cooled off? Are you now serving Him and want to assure that you will never backslide? Do you have family or friends who are backslidden or unchurched? Then this book is for you! Its contents will help you or someone you care about find the way home.

The Captain's Mantle

Something happened in the cave Adullum. Find out how 400 distressed, indebted, and discontented men came out of that cave as one of the most awesome armies in history!

MANUALS

Ministry of Helps

Ministry of Helps is a companion manual to the Minister's Manual and was written to help pastors, ministers, administrators, and other leaders to establish a strong and effective ministry of helps in the local church. Topics include training and qualifications, organization, communications, church leadership, having church, and more.

Minister's Manual

Minister's Manual is a companion manual to Ministry of Helps and was written with the specific needs of ministers in mind. Topics include ethics, governments, administration, building a ministry of helps, the local church, sacraments, pastoring the local church, executives, protocol, the supernatural and the practical, and more.

SERIES

Entire selection of series on CD, DVD, USB, and Digital Downloads are available at *www.marktbarclay.com*.

How to Study Your Bible (CD or DVD)

In this powerful series, Brother Barclay offers three teachings on this vital topic. The first two titles cover how to study your Bible personally and at church. The third message offers insight into tools to help you study your Bible.

SUPERNATURAL MINISTRIES TRAINING INSTITUTE (SMTI)

"Building Believers for Ministry"

SMTI is a contemporary ministry training institute, specializing in spiritual Bible training—building, developing, and equipping believers with the Scriptures to function supernaturally in all areas of ministry. SMTI presents the uncompromised, practical, life-adjusting Word of God in a straightforward, understandable format that is applicable for a wide range of individuals (lay people as well as full-time ministers). SMTI designs and presents scriptural curriculum in a way that builds character, imparts vision, and provides insight about the end times—causing believers and churches to flourish and courageously climax the ages.

CURRICULUM

The SMTI curriculum includes three different courses of study. Each course is designed to be completed in a nine-month period (31 weeks of teachings). All classes are taught by Mark T. Barclay.

Supernatural Helps

Supernatural Helps is designed to build character, help define and perfect the call on an individual's life, and develop supportive ministries in the local church.

Advanced Survival Techniques

Advanced Survival Techniques is designed to help the end-time leaders and believers in dealing with the crucial matters of life and ministry.

Ministerial Practicalities

Ministerial Practicalities will provide practical training about the local church, administration, legalities, ceremonies, executive ethics, and wisdom to perform with excellence in the ministry.